Contents

Lots of Colors

HOUGHTON MIFFLIN   BOSTON

Printed in China

ISBN-13: 978-0-618-93122-4
ISBN-10: 0-618-93122-8

1 2 3 4 5 6 7 8 9 SDP 15 14 13 12 11 10 09 08

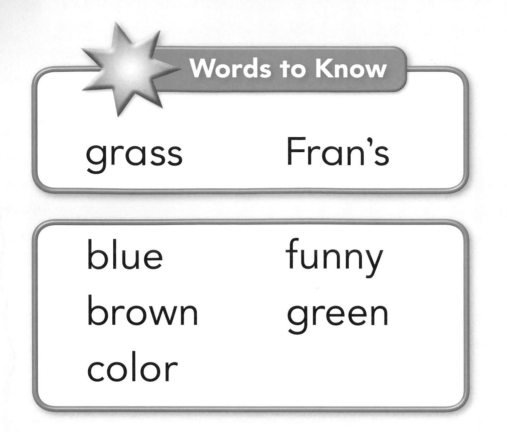

Words to Know

grass   Fran's

blue   funny

brown   green

color

Colors

by Carol Hindin

Is grass green?   Yes!

Is mud brown? Yes!

Is Fran's funny hat red?   Yes!

What color is the sun?
Is it blue? Never!

let's   Fred

Brad's   grab

also   blue

likes   green

many   funny

some

Fred's Hats

by Carol Hindin

illustrated by Jannie Ho

Fred likes some blue hats.

Fred also likes green hats.

Fred's many hats fell!
Let's grab his hats.

Fred gets Brad's funny hat.